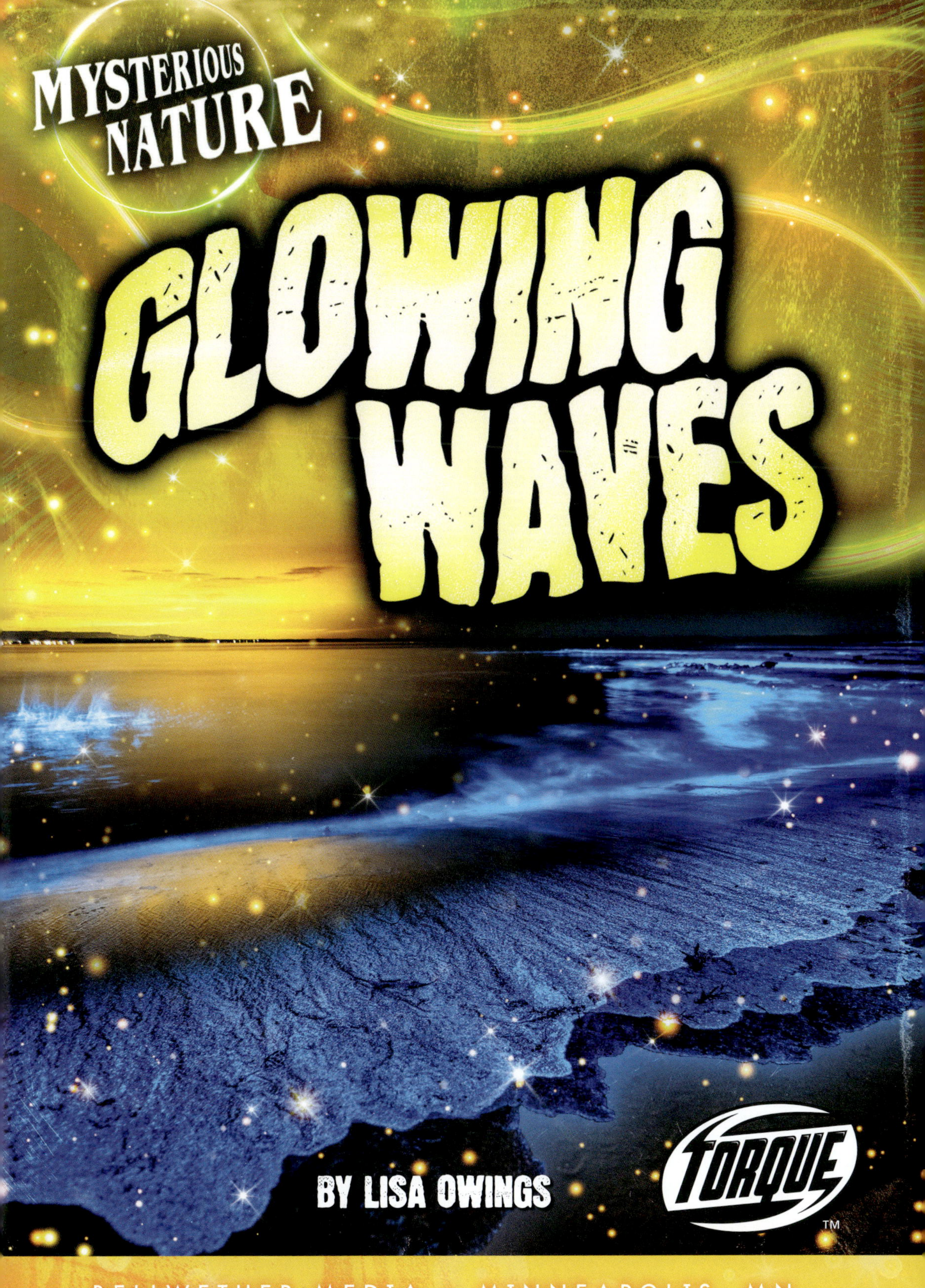

BELLWETHER MEDIA • MINNEAPOLIS, MN

Torque brims with excitement perfect for thrill-seekers of all kinds. Discover daring survival skills, explore uncharted worlds, and marvel at mighty engines and extreme sports. In *Torque* books, anything can happen. Are you ready?

This edition first published in 2025 by Bellwether Media, Inc.

Library of Congress Cataloging-in-Publication Data

LC record for Glowing Waves available at: https://lccn.loc.gov/2024009419

Editor: Rebecca Sabelko   Designer: Josh Brink

Printed in the United States of America, North Mankato, MN.

TABLE OF CONTENTS

The Blue Bay

The sunset casts a warm light over the bay. Beachgoers watch the Sun go down. They are waiting for the real show to begin. The bay will glow after dark!

Each wave is edged in a blue glow. Glowing trails follow people moving in the water. The bay fills with blue light with each footstep and splash!

What Are Glowing Waves?

Glowing waves are displays of **bioluminescence**. They happen in ocean waters filled with tiny **organisms** called **dinoflagellates**. Each dinoflagellate gives off its own light. Large groups of them give the water a blue-green glow at night.

dinoflagellate

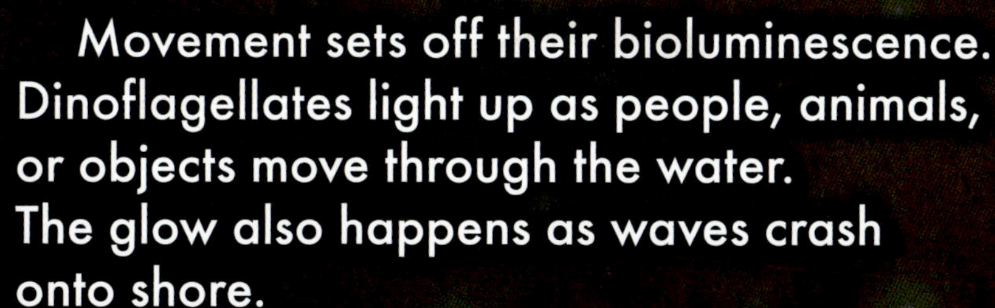

Movement sets off their bioluminescence. Dinoflagellates light up as people, animals, or objects move through the water. The glow also happens as waves crash onto shore.

Bioluminescence in Nature

firefly

jack-o'-lantern mushroom

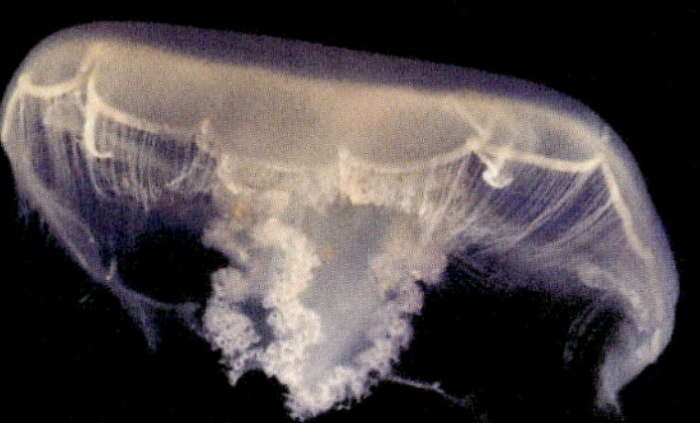

crystal jellyfish

anglerfish

Glowing waves exist year-round in just a few places on Earth. These places are called bioluminescent bays, or bio bays.

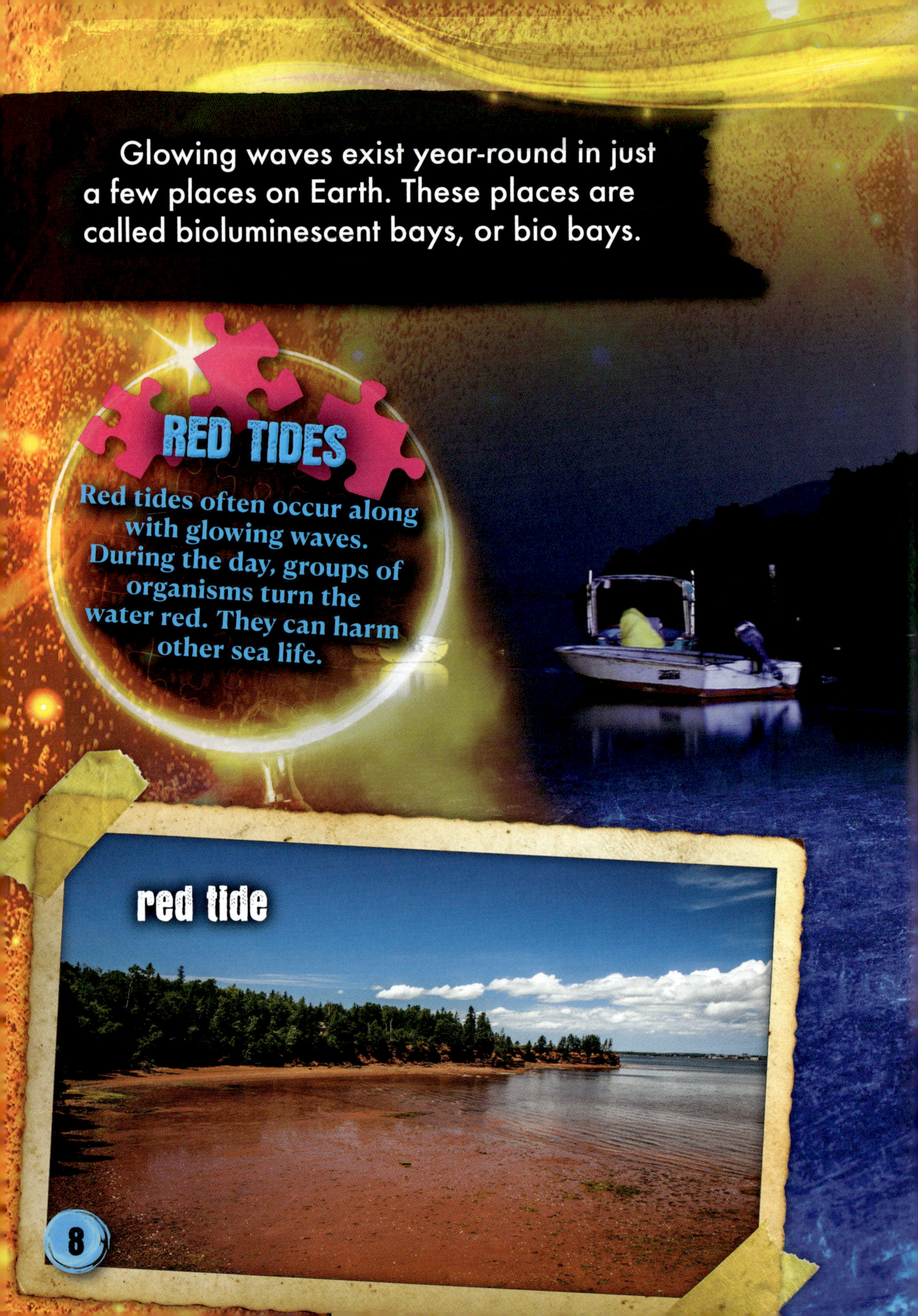

RED TIDES

Red tides often occur along with glowing waves. During the day, groups of organisms turn the water red. They can harm other sea life.

Bio bays form in calm, **tropical** waters. Dinoflagellates get trapped in bio bays. Their numbers grow. They cause entire bays to light up! Glowing waves can also occur along coasts in cooler regions during summer.

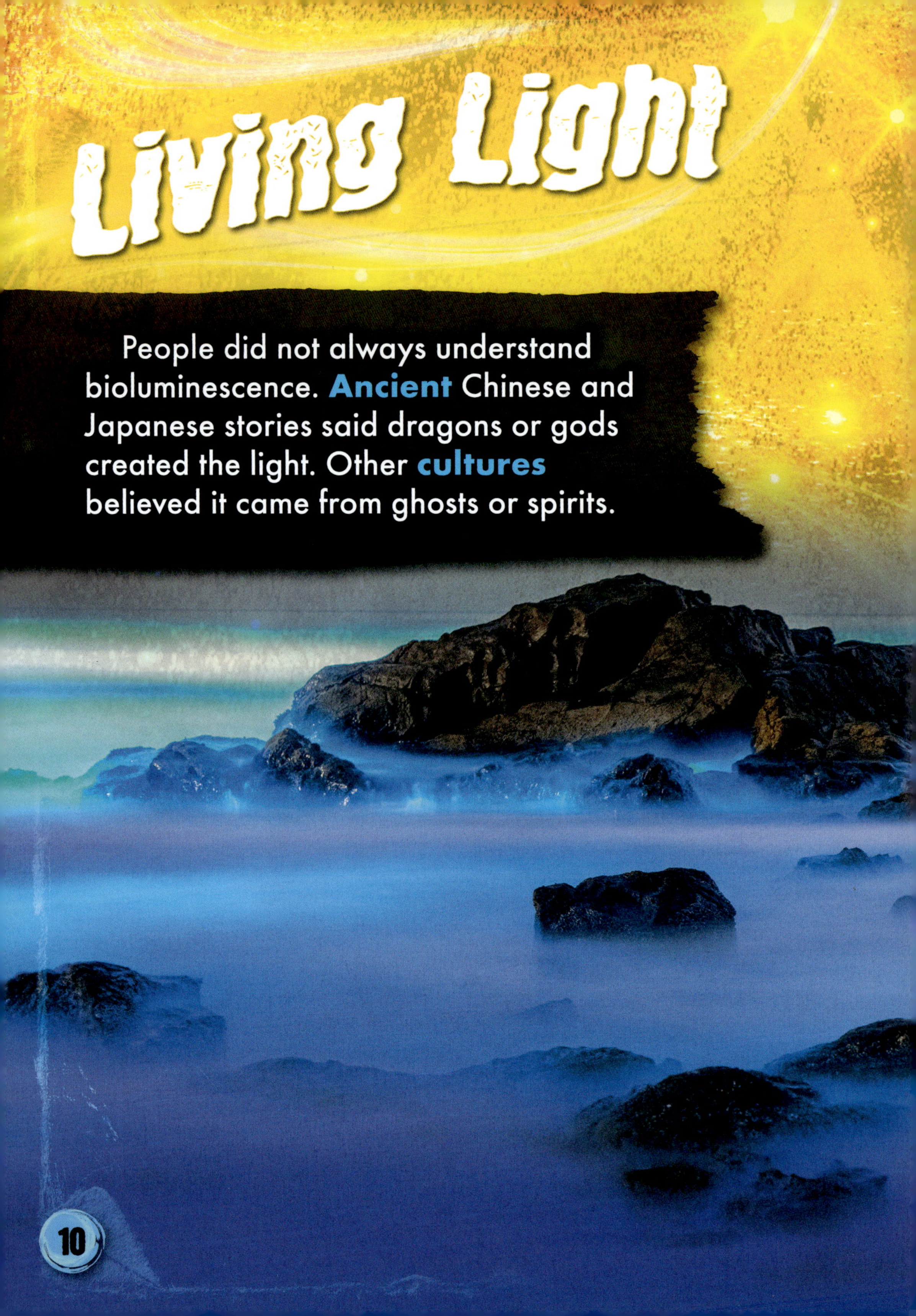

Living Light

People did not always understand bioluminescence. **Ancient** Chinese and Japanese stories said dragons or gods created the light. Other **cultures** believed it came from ghosts or spirits.

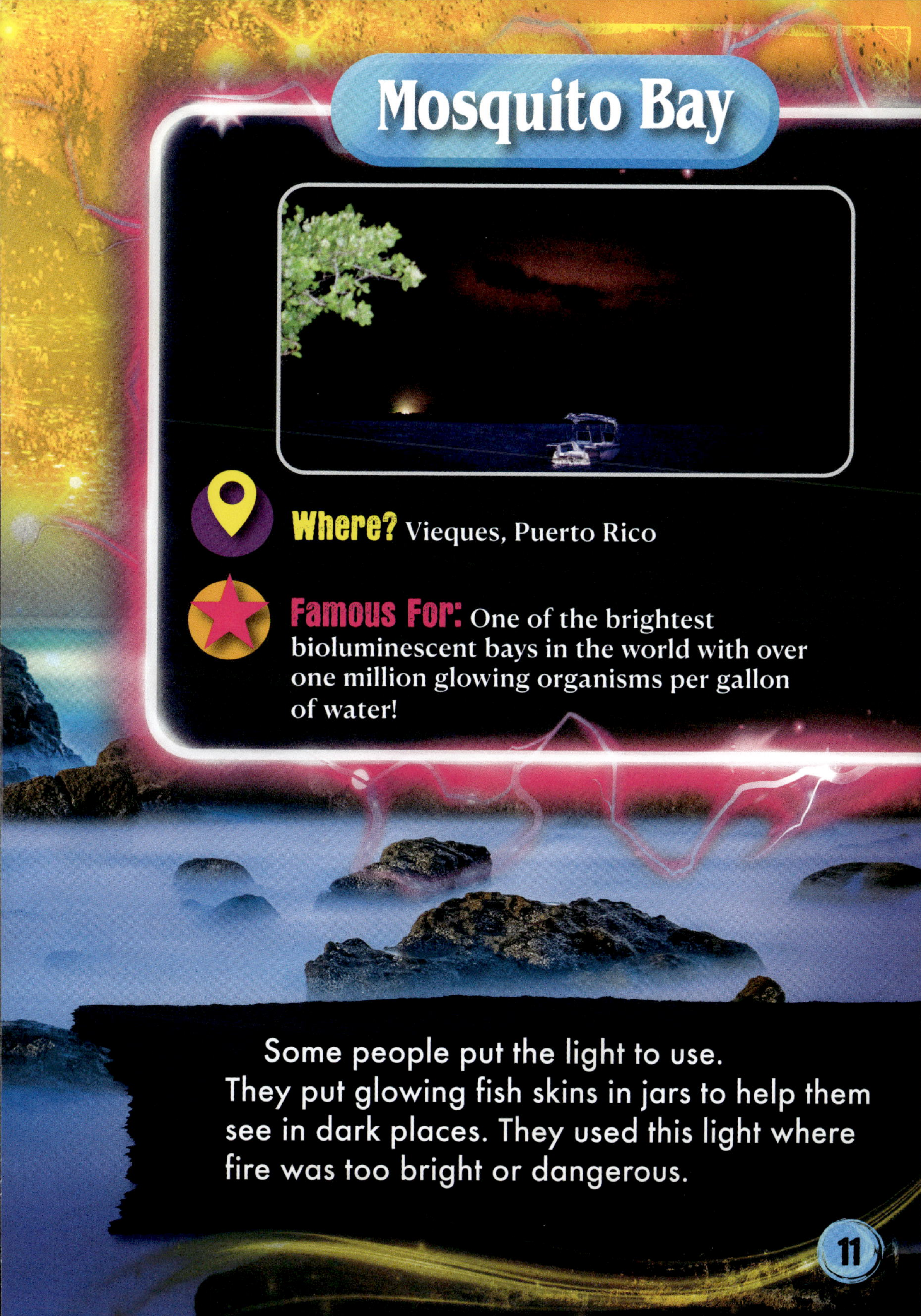

Mosquito Bay

Where? Vieques, Puerto Rico

Famous For: One of the brightest bioluminescent bays in the world with over one million glowing organisms per gallon of water!

Some people put the light to use. They put glowing fish skins in jars to help them see in dark places. They used this light where fire was too bright or dangerous.

Aristotle wrote about bioluminescence in the 300s BCE. He noted that the light was cold. It came from within living things.

Sailors who explored the seas during the **Middle Ages** told of burning seas. Scientists became more interested in studying glowing waves during this time. In 1753 CE, Benjamin Franklin guessed glowing water came from tiny animals.

statue of Aristotle

Benjamin Franklin
HIDE AND SEEK
Glowing waters make it hard for ships to hide. Navy ships must avoid glowing waves if they want to stay hidden from enemies.

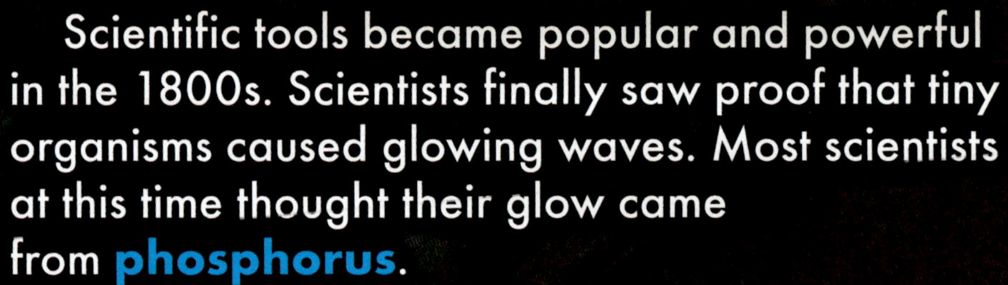

Scientific tools became popular and powerful in the 1800s. Scientists finally saw proof that tiny organisms caused glowing waves. Most scientists at this time thought their glow came from **phosphorus**.

Phosphorescence

Before Dubois, most scientists thought phosphorus made organisms glow. Phosphorus is a material that absorbs light. It then glows in the dark. It is used to make glow-in-the-dark objects.

glow toy

glow stick

Raphaël Dubois proved that idea wrong. He found that glowing organisms create their own light.

Raphaël Dubois

Glow Science

Bioluminescence is a **chemical reaction**. Light is made when an **enzyme** combines with oxygen inside a **luciferin**. The reaction makes a bright glow with almost no heat.

In most glowing waves, this reaction happens within dinoflagellates. They glow when they sense motion. The glow fades in less than a second when their chemicals are used up. Their chemicals recharge the next day. They can glow again!

The Science of Bioluminescence

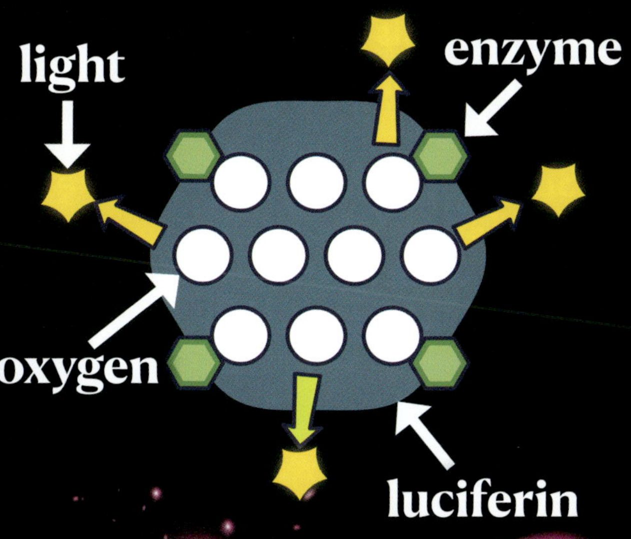

Bioluminescence is common in ocean waters. Some animals use it to get food. It also helps them find **mates**. Some use it to send messages.

Scientists think dinoflagellates glow to stay safe. The glow may keep enemies away. Dinoflagellates are less likely to be eaten. They live to glow another day!

bioluminescent animal

WHY SO BLUE?

Blue is the most common color in bioluminescence. Blue light travels the farthest in water.

Scientists are studying how to protect bio bays from **climate change**. Strong storms and washed-up seaweed can harm them.

But these bays can heal. Some have come back brighter, even after major tropical storms. With luck, glowing waves will continue to light up the night!

GLOSSARY

ancient—from long ago

bioluminescence—light produced by living things

chemical reaction—a change that occurs when two or more substances mix to form a new substance

climate change—a human-caused change in Earth's weather due to warming temperatures

cultures—societies that hold the same beliefs, arts, and ways of life

dinoflagellates—one-celled organisms that live in the sea

enzyme—a substance made by a living thing that causes chemical reactions to happen faster within the living thing

luciferin—a substance that produces light when it combines with oxygen

mates—adult animals that produce offspring

Middle Ages—the period of European history from about 500 to 1500 CE

organisms—living things

phosphorus—a chemical element that glows in the dark

tropical—related to the tropics; the tropics is a hot, rainy region near the equator.

TO LEARN MORE

AT THE LIBRARY

Bioluminescent Animals. London, U.K.: DK Children, 2023.

Kuo, Julia. *Luminous: Living Things That Light Up the Night.* Vancouver, B.C.: Greystone Books, 2022.

Smith, Jennifer. *Glow.* New York, N.Y.: Thames & Hudson Inc., 2023.

ON THE WEB

FACTSURFER

Factsurfer.com gives you a safe, fun way to find more information.

1. Go to www.factsurfer.com
2. Enter "glowing waves" into the search box and click 🔍.
3. Select your book cover to see a list of related content.

INDEX

The images in this book are reproduced through the courtesy of: Petar Belobrajdic/ Getty Images, front cover (hero); Tharuka Photographer, pp. 2-3, 4-5, 22-24; hor division, CSIRO/ Wiki Commons, p. 6 (dinoflagellate); RugliG, pp. 6-7; HHelen, p. 7 (firefly); milart, p. 7 (jack-o'-lantern mushroom); Klittinit Yassara, p. 7 (crystal jellyfish); Doug Perrine/ Alamy, p. 7 (anglerfish); smcfeeters, p. 8 (red tide); Joe Chen Photography/ Getty Images, pp. 8-9; Kenvin Key/ SIworking/ Getty Images, pp. 10-11; Edgar Torres/ Wiki Commons, p. 11; Andrejs Marcenko, p. 12 (statue of Aristotle); Joseph Duplessisc. 1785/ Google Cultural Institute/ Wiki Commons, p. 13 (Benjamin Franklin); Ting Cheng, pp. 12-13; Wayne Carter Photography, p. 14 (glow toy); Vladimir_Zhukov, p. 14 (glow stick); Associated Press/ AP Newsroom, pp. 14-15; Veronidae/ Wiki Commons, p. 15 (Raphaël Dubois); Preetham Udyavara, pp. 16-17; VectorMine, p. 17; shunli zhao/ Getty Images, pp. 18-19; Diego Grandi, p. 19; Candyfloss-Film/ Getty Images, pp. 20-21; Tharuka Wanniarachchi, back cover.